Samue

How To Deal With Social Anxiety

Step-by-step guide to conquering social anxiety disorder

2015

Disclaimer

The information provided herein is stated to be truthful and consistent, in that any liability, in terms of inattention or otherwise, by any usage or abuse of any policies, processes, or directions contained within is the solitary and utter responsibility of the recipient reader. Under no circumstances will any legal responsibility or blame be held against the publisher for any reparation, damages, or monetary loss due to the information herein, either directly or indirectly.

The information herein is offered for informational purposes solely, and is universal as so. The presentation of the information is without contract or any type of guarantee assurance.

The trademarks that are used are without any consent, and the publication of the trademark is without permission or backing by the trademark owner. All trademarks and brands within this book are for clarifying purposes only and are owned by the owners themselves, not affiliated with this document.

Introduction

While, of course, all children have moments of irrational shyness, for the majority, childhood is a time blissfully unburdened by inhibitions. As young children, we were able to play, learn, grow and simply be, without worrying about what others thought. As we get older, though, many of us lose the ability to fully embrace life because we become overly aware of the opinions of others.

Have you ever felt nervous for no reason other than the fact that you are entering a social situation?

Do you become self conscious and uncomfortable when you are surrounded by people?

When out in public, do you imagine that people are watching and judging you?

Do you get anxious when approaching the till in a shop or ordering food?

Are you awkward around people that you do not know well?

Do you feel as though you are not as good as other people?

Are you terrified of talking in front of a group of people?

If you are answering yes to some or all of these questions, the first thing to realize is that you are not alone. Social anxiety affects millions of people all over the world, and it is caused by factors beyond your control (yes, that does mean that your social anxiety is not your fault). The next thing to realize is that while social anxiety can be extremely hard to deal with, no matter how severe it is, it can be managed, and eventually overcome. So, the final thing to realize here is that you have done the right thing by getting this book. It was a brave move, and by deciding you want to address your social anxiety you have taken the first step towards taking control of your life. Take a minute to applaud yourself, seriously, you deserve it, and, as cheesy as it may sound, you should feel good about it.

The reason you should feel good about yourself for getting this book is because it works. This is a step-by-step guide that will help you first to understand social anxiety, and then to overcome it. It includes reliable statistics and real life personal stories bravely shared by people who have dealt with struggles that are probably similar to the ones you are facing, so that you know you are not alone in feeling alone. And, it offers practical advice, motivation, tasks and activities that will help you to recover your true sense of self.

In short, you have just embarked on a journey that will change your life for the better. In the pages that follow, you will learn to master the fear that is currently holding you back. Consider the factual information, take on board the advice and embrace what this book offers... to do so is to embrace life.

Defining the Problem

Humans are social creatures. In fact, it is the very reason that our ancient ancestors were able to survive the harsh world in which they lived; They learned to work together in order to overcome great obstacles. Developing these key communication skills was fundamental not only to the survival of our primate predecessors, but to their evolution as well. As our forerunners developed communication skills, they also, necessarily, developed the very thing that distinguished them from all other animals, intelligent consciousness. It is no great leap, therefore, to understand that socializing is at the very heart of what makes us human.

An ability to mix with others is not something that has outrun its use. In the modern age, while the need to work together in order to survive predators is no more, we still do exist as a community. And, all of the logistics aside, we need social interaction if we are to be truly content in our lives. We have all heard the famous quote; "*Happiness is only real when it is shared*", but to really appreciate how integral other people are to our own well being, consider the wise words of the Dalai Lama:

"We human beings are social beings. We come into the world as the result of others' actions. We survive here in dependence on others. Whether we like it or not, there is hardly a moment of our lives when we

do not benefit from others' activities. For this reason, it is hardly surprising that most of our happiness arises in the context of our relationships with others."

Yet, despite all of this scientific proof and insightful philosophy, there are many of us in the world today who are experiencing a reduced quality of life because we suffer from some form of social anxiety. These issues arise without invitation, and can prevent us from reaching our full potential. Often the fears and fixations seem illogical, but there is reasoning behind them, and once you see this, you can begin to take control.

What is Social Anxiety?

Social anxiety disorder, also known as social phobia, is a broad term for a certified anxiety disorder that affects people in varying degrees. It is characterized by an extreme and irrational fear of social situations, intense nervousness when dealing with other people and a heightened, inhibiting sense of self consciousness. Oftentimes, sufferer's concerns will be compounded by the fact that, due to the nature of the condition, they will not have developed social skills and may lack experience in dealing with others.

Simply put, social anxiety is a severely debilitating emotional problem that can ruin many of the moments that make up a life. Instead of enjoying mixing with others, people with social anxiety are concerned with being humiliated and talked about by others. They strive to just get through social events, in some cases avoiding them all together, and thus, missing out on potential experiences.

However, it is not just a nervousness when faced with social situations, social anxiety can also cause:

- **Panic Attacks:** Sudden, overwhelming and debilitatingly intense bouts of anxiety that occur without any real threat. They result from a misfiring adrenaline reaction, and therefore, are not your fault.
- **Distorted Thinking:** Imaging that others do not like you, and, in turn, cultivating unfairly negative opinions of them.
- **Anticipatory Anxiety:** Fearing situations before they even happen and feeling excessively nervous in the days/weeks leading up to the event, despite knowing that this is illogical.
- **Feelings of Inferiority:** Believing that you are worthless, or simply not as good as others and unable to achieve the same things that they can, despite the fact that this is not true.

And, a fear of the following:

- Getting work done in front of other people
- Eating/drinking around others
- Having people focus their attention on you
- Talking in a group of people
- Passing by a group of people when out in public
- Talking on the phone
- Talking on Skype
- Using public bathrooms, or the toilets in the homes of friends/relatives

Symptoms of Social Anxiety

In extreme cases, the effects of social anxiety are so obvious that the sufferer is acutely aware exactly what the problem is, but for many, there is just an underlying feeling that something is wrong. The condition is linked to a number of other mental illnesses, including depression and obsessive compulsive disorder, and a large number of people seek medical help for these issues before realizing that anxiety is at the root of their troubles.

There are a number of common symptoms relating to social anxiety that can be easy to miss. These include:

- Confusion
- Awkwardness
- An inability to concentrate
- Increase of heart beat
- Heavily pounding heart
- Feeling tense
- Blushing
- Sweating
- Shaking
- Dry throat
- Feeling sick in your stomach
- Loss of appetite
- Diarrhea

Effects of Social Anxiety

We have outlined the physical and mental symptoms and effects of social anxiety, but now, lets think long term. Not only are you suffering on a daily basis, but you are suffering in terms of your life as a whole as well. Consider these knock on effects of social anxiety, and you will soon be determined to control the condition before it controls you.

Isolation: Right now, you may feel nervous about mixing with people, and therefore you may not want to do it. You may have trouble connecting with others, even close family and friends. It might not seem like it, but think, are you able to listen to others and advise them, but unable to open up in the same way? One of the most common complaints of people who struggle like this, and who never learn to communicate their feelings openly and honestly to others, is a profound sense of loneliness that haunts them, particularly as they get older. Even the famously isolated writer Charles Bukowski admitted that this is no way to live, saying, towards the end of his life, that *"Being alone never felt right. Sometimes it felt good, but it never felt right".*

Constant Fear: If you suffer from social anxiety, you are probably well used to regular bouts of nervousness. You probably deal with these as best as you can, by avoiding them or taking other temporary measures, but these are only short term solutions. Imagine if you let this continue; Aside from the countless missed experiences, you do not want to look back at your life in years to come and realize that you have eked out an existence in a state of perpetual fear. It is no way to live, so don't resign yourself to it.

Alcohol/Drug Dependency: It is not uncommon for people with social anxiety to self medicate with alcohol and drugs when their condition goes undiagnosed. The reason for this is simple: Alcohol and drugs create pleasurable chemical reactions in the mind and lower inhibitions. However, the problems this can lead to are complex, and, while they are not advisory anyway, when you are using alcohol or dugs as a coping mechanism you are in trouble. Be careful if this is something that you do, history is littered with sensitive people who have had their lives destroyed by addiction.

Lost Relationships: Social anxiety can make it extremely hard to meet new people. Even if you would like to talk to someone, and know that you would get on well with them, the condition can, quite literally, be a barrier that prevents you from connecting with others. You may be too nervous to even initiate a conversation or, if you so manage that, you might be too anxious to really be yourself when talking. This means that others will not get to know you, and you will lose out on potentially rewarding long lasting friendships.

Missed Opportunities: Many people who suffer from social anxiety feel that it has not only impeded their relationships with others, but that it has cost them successful careers as well. There are countless horror stories of people turning down big promotions because they were too afraid to accept the new responsibilities, and of others who are unable to work at all simply because they are too terrified. The sad truth is, everybody has potential inside them and, luck aside, audacity is one of the key ingredients to success. In other (unfortunate) words, it is true what they say; Victory favours the brave.

How To Deal With Social Anxiety

Ultimately, long term sufferers of social anxiety experience very low levels of life satisfaction. After many years of hiding themselves away, they are plagued by regrets and frustrated with what they have (or, perhaps more accurately, have not) achieved, and are often lonely and unfulfilled.

If this sounds like something that could happen to you, or indeed, something that has happened to you, do not despair. It needs not to be your fate forever, this book is specifically designed to help you.

Understanding the Problem

Before we can start thinking about how to overcome social anxiety, it is first necessary to reach a further understanding of the condition itself. A more comprehensive knowledge of the full scope of anxiety, including related statistics, personal accounts and how the problem is developing in the digital age, will help to take the mystery away from the misery and the power away from the problem.

Social Anxiety: A Brief History

While we tend to think of social anxiety as a modern disorder, it has actually been affecting people for thousands of years. Believe it or not, the feelings that many people experience today were also documented in Roman civilization, and writings from as early as 400 BC describe the struggles of overly shy men as a plight that causes them to "think that every man observes them".

Sounds Familiar?

While there have been hundreds of famous historical figures who have suffered from bouts of anxiety (including Abraham Lincoln), it wasn't until the early 20th century that psychiatrists began to understand that extremely shy patients were suffering from a form of social phobia. And, it wasn't for over 50 years that they began to think of this as something more complex than other phobias.

In the 1980's, the Diagnostic and Statistical Manual of Mental Disorders included social phobia as an official psychiatric diagnosis, however, this offered a narrow definition of the condition and it wasn't until 1994 that the term Social Anxiety Disorder was introduced. Social Anxiety Disorder (or, yes, SAD) is a term that was coined in order to reflect the broad scope of fears caused by the illness can cause. Since the introduction of this as a diagnostic term, a vast amount of research has been done to correct the idea that social anxiety is the least understood and most common form of anxiety.

Related Anxieties

Apart from the fact that no one who hasn't experienced social anxiety could ever start to imagine what it feels like, one of the key reasons that the condition had been misunderstood for so long is that it can include a number of other disorders as well. See if anything from the following list resonates with you, if so, realizing the full extent of your struggle will help you to deal with it.

- **Agoraphobia:** Fear of being in a public place where an unnoticed escape would be difficult.
- **Generalized Anxiety Disorder:** Anxiousness at the result of being faced with various situations or objects, without any apparent connection or reason.
- **Obsessive Compulsive Disorder:** Anxiety manifesting itself in the form of obsessive thoughts and compulsive behaviors.
- **Panic Disorder:** Experiencing panic attacks as a result of certain situations, feelings or thoughts, including fear of having another panic attack.
- **Post-traumatic Stress Disorder:** Anxiety recurring as the result of a specific trauma.
- **Social Phobia:** Once thought to be the only form of social anxiety; relates to anxiety caused by public performances/speaking and a fear of being humiliated.
- **Specific Phobia:** Anxiety caused by a specific situation or object.

The Facts and Figures

The sad fact is that social anxiety is the least acknowledged form of anxiety, and this is made even worse by another fact; it is one of the most common forms of anxiety. It is the third most common mental health care problem in the world today.

According to social anxiety institute over 8% of the worlds population suffers from some form of the social anxiety. That means that a staggering 560,000 million people feel isolated and share the same struggles as you. So, all over the world, there are thousands of healthy looking people visiting doctors and saying things like: *"Every time I go out I feel that people are staring at me"*, *"I'm too nervous around people to really open up and be my true self"*, *"I dread social events that I cannot avoid, for weeks before they happen"* and *"Whenever people focus their attention on me I get scared"*.

Social anxiety is equally common in men and women, however, women are more likely to receive treatment, and therefore, women are more likely to conquer the condition. And, while the most common age for sufferers to begin showing symptoms is 13, the illness has a lifetime prevalence rate of 14%, so it can occur long after the formative teenage years.

There is effective treatment available, but despite this, surveys have shown that people struggle with social anxiety for an average of ten years before finally deciding to get help. Even more surprisingly, the vast majority (two thirds, in fact) of people who suffer with social anxiety do so in silence. Instead of taking action, they accept an unsatisfying life in a state of perpetual nervousness.

Statistics aside, the key facts are these: Yes, social anxiety is a severe disorder that can negatively affect pretty much every aspect of your life, but it is treatable. You are not alone in feeling the way that you do, millions of others feel the same way, and, those who seek help, do overcome it.

Social Anxiety Today

Today, social anxiety is more understood than ever before. This means that psychiatrists and doctors are better equipped to properly diagnose and treat the disorder than they have ever been, and, that guides like this book can offer practical and proven advice. On the other side of the spectrum, however, is the fact that these treatments are more necessary today than ever because the percentage of people who struggle with social anxiety and related mental illnesses is rapidly increasing.

While social anxiety itself is a relatively recent term, and so, its diagnosis rate is hard to chart accurately, according to American health care reports; "The amount of people who are so severely disabled by anxiety disorders that they rely on social welfare payments to survive has increased by nearly two and a half times between 1987 and 2007". Of course, these worrying figures relate specifically to America, but similar rates of increase have occurred in the majority of developed countries. There are a number of reasons for this, including added social/professional pressures and expectations, but the most prominent factor in the ever increasing number of people suffering from social anxiety is digitalization. This is directly responsible for the alarmingly high percentage of children who have been diagnosed with the disorder, and for the continued growth in numbers since 2007.

For many, leisure time now centres around television and computer games rather than social events. That is not to knock watching a bit of TV or playing computer games, but the dangers of spending excessive amounts of time isolated in front of a screen are real. Many of the teenagers who suffer from social anxiety today do so as a result of underdeveloped social skills. And, as fun as computer games are, they do not encourage socializing. Think about it, the more you do something, the better you get at it, so children, and indeed, teenagers/adults, who rely on gaming as their primary recreational activity do so at the expense of interacting face to face with others, and therefore their ability to mix suffers. And, creating a comfort zone where you are alone means that you will be nervous when leaving it and going out in public.

If you like to play games and watch TV, that is fine, but try to do so with friends as much as possible. In fact, these can be excellent bonding experiences. If someone you know is interested in the same game or show as you, talk to them about it. You now have some common ground to break the ice, and eventually, you can invite them over to play said game or watch the show. This will make things more enjoyable, and will help you develop social skills and friendships, and remember, talking to people over a headset while you play does not count!

Not only do we have anti-social hobbies in the modern age, we also have anti-social means of socializing. Instead of communicating and talking with people face to face, we now do so via computers and smartphones. People say what they need over platforms like Facebook, or through email and text, and do not actually talk to each other directly. On top of this, constant connection means that there is no real chance for people to switch off when they come home. Instead of relaxing and refreshing ourselves, many of us waste hours online looking at unrepresentative pictures of others and viewing their conversations and life events. Again, this is not all negative, social media is an excellent and affordable way of keeping up to date with friends across the world, but it should not be your primary means of communication. It may sound harsh, but if you feel more comfortable texting or messaging someone than you do actually talking to them, you may have a problem.

You should limit the control that social media has over your life by controlling the amount of time you spend on it each day, only being friends with people who you would actually say hello to if you passed in the street and trying to talk or Skype rather than text or instant message.

Socially Anxious or Just Shy?

Social anxiety can cause people to be extremely nervous when mixing with others and to want to avoid social situations. Shyness, however... can cause people to want to avoid social situations and to be extremely nervous when mixing with others.

Understandably, the two are often thought of as interlinked, and have even been confused for each other, but the truth is, they are two completely different things.

Shyness is a personality trait. Some shy people do feel that their bashful disposition is something that is holding them back and therefore would find the advice in this book beneficial, but many others are content because they do not suffer from the negative emotions and distorted thinking that accompany social anxiety disorder, and, thus, live rich and happy lives. Shyness then, is not something that requires treatment or needs fixing, it can, in fact, be a very endearing quality.

Social anxiety disorder, on the other hand, is a debilitating mental condition. It is not a reflection of the sufferer's personality. While some people with the disorder are also naturally shy, an equal amount (literally, half the amount of diagnoses!) are extroverted people who have been affected by an illness, but who will once again enjoy being the centre of attention after they get some help. People suffering from social anxiety come from all sorts of different backgrounds, but they have one thing in common; they have a disorder that is ruining their lives.

Still unsure of the difference between being shy and having social anxiety? Think about it like this: A shy person probably wouldn't want to become/enjoy being a TV talk show host, whereas a person suffering from social anxiety might have already been enjoying that career before developing the condition, and may be dreaming of making a big comeback as soon as they recover.

Social Anxiety in Society

"It never leaves, it never lets up. It is constant. It is lurking. It is fear, anxiety, pain, self loathing, frustration, dejection and avoidance. It is a feeling of "I can't do that because..." or "I could do that too, if only...". It is panic when entering a conversation that you feel you are not capable of maintaining. It is the voice inside your head that removes you from the moment and stops you from enjoying what you were doing. The one that says: "That was a stupid thing to say" or "They're laughing at you, not with you" or "Somebody else would be handing this situation so much better".

It is hiding the real you and not embracing the life you could live. It is not doing what you want to do or saying what you want to say. It is the unnamed reason you feel different.

It is the dirty secret that you hide from others; the one you put up walls to protect and the one that you carry around always."

That is the haunting attempt of a person with social anxiety disorder to describe the condition. The reference to the disorder as *"it"* is particularly telling, as most sufferer's believe that they are burdened with a fatal flaw which prevents them from living a normal life, but which also must be hidden away from others. This conveys how the disorder feels, but consider these brave accounts that detail the effects of social anxiety in every day situations:

"I am the person who dreads going to the grocery store. As I shop, I let others reach ahead of me and take items I want, even if I have been there first and they are the last in stock. The others deserve it more, they will do something better with the ingredients. When I do pick up something ahead of someone else, I feel like a spoilt child that has pathetically collected up all its toys. I am apologetic and embarrassed even to be there. If I can't find something, I usually don't get it, and when I do bother a member of staff from their more important work, I feel like a nuisance. When people bang into me, I blush and say sorry. In my mind, they are all watching me and judging me as inferior. I worry about where to go as I push my trolley, I don't turn back when I have missed something. My heart pounds as I stand in line for the till. I haven't gotten everything I wanted, but there is no turning around now. My groceries are a joke, I have picked laughable food. I mumble weakly in response to the cashier, fidget around pathetically for my money, and hold up everyone else as I fumble with my shopping bags."

"I am the student that misses college when there is going to be a presentation, even if I know I will lose marks because of it. Public speaking makes me feel sick; it makes my throat dry up and my stomach ache. It makes me sweat and makes my heart race . I avoid picking modules that have presentations as part of the course work, and when one is announced as a surprise, I panic about it for days. Sometimes I

can't eat and the night before I can't sleep. My presentation slides are excellent, I compensate for my lack of speaking skills with detailed work and I enjoy doing it, but I get tongue tied and flustered when the lecturer asks me a question, so how could I stand up in front of everyone and talk? It makes my work completely worthless. Not only that, but I'll never be able to get a job that involves presentations or speaking in front of a group, even though I want to share my work with people. It's infuriating. I feel like a failure."

"I'm a young professional in a new city. I have never found it very easy to make friends, but now I am extremely lonely. At least at home I had my family, but here I don't know anyone at all. My colleagues are nice, but we never really connect at work. They seem to have a lot of fun together though, and they invite me to parties regularly. I would like to go and have a real conversation with someone, but I can't bring myself to do it. The thought of so many people in one place terrifies me. It was hard enough meeting people at work when I could escape to my desk. Even though I long for companionship, the thought of being around them and being introduced to their friends on a night with nothing else to do makes me panic. Even though that is what I want to do. They might be nice to my face, but they will soon realize that I am boring and insignificant. I'll be rejected, and people will laugh at me. No one will want to talk to me, and even if they did, I'd soon run out of things to talk about. I'd be uncomfortable and out of place if I go, so I'll just stay in my apartment and watch TV Again."

Here, we have three different accounts that attest to various symptoms and consequences, with regard to specific situations. The first person is so self conscious and insecure that he is embarrassed even to go to the grocery store and buy the food he needs to survive. He lets others take precedent over him, and feels guilty if he ever does the same. Even when he has forgotten items, he is too inhibited to go back ad get them. This is because he imagines that everyone is watching him, when in reality everyone is just doing their own shopping. Similarly, he imagines that people are annoyed at him for holding them up at the till, when, really, he is taking just as much time as everyone else does. And, if he ever does take longer, it is because he has gotten himself so worked about taking a long time packing his bags that he panics and then actually does a long time packing his bags.

In the next account, we have a student who is painfully aware of how he is sabotaging himself. His social anxiety is preventing him from talking in public, to the point where he actually chooses the classes that have the least amount of presentations, even if they are boring. And, when these modules do occasionally call for public speaking, he panics, and then simply does not attend. He prepares what he feels is very good work, but it is all in vain because he will not get any marks if he doesn't share it with the class. His frustration is understandable; if things continue the way they are, he knows his future career will be limited.

Finally, we have a scarily simple account of how someone with social anxiety can become increasingly isolated. The young woman has moved to a new city for work, but is unable to connect. She has no network of support to encourage her to go out and socialize, and therefore is inclined to reject her work-mates offers. Not only does this mean that she doesn't go out and get to know them, it means that they will eventually stop inviting her. Her existence, then, will continue to be one of extreme loneli-ness, void of any sort of social interaction beyond superficial ones at work. And, ironically, these could probably develop into something more meaningful if she was able to go to one of the parties with her workmates.

Taking Control

The above accounts may sound familiar, but they don't sound very fun. Nobody wants to be governed by a disorder, especially not one that can easily be treated. Why feel like you are worth less than everyone else or spend your time lost inside your mind, unable to enjoy life, when you can get help? Unless you want to continue living in fear, frustration or isolation, those should be hard questions to answer.

Have you ever felt as self conscious and embarrassed as the man above when going to a grocery store or somewhere similar? Or, are you frustrated and risking your future career, or even worse, happiness and relationships, because of your inhibitions?

If so, or indeed, even if you are just overly shy and would like to improve your social skills, then congratulations. By reaching an understanding of social anxiety, you are now ready to re-train your mind and take control over your life.

You're about to make a drastic change, and that is a good thing. As the timeless warning goes: *"Do not live the same year 85 times and call it a life"*.

The First Steps of Recovery

Commitment

Technically, just by buying this book you have taken the first step towards recovery. And by reaching an understanding of social anxiety disorder you have provided yourself with the foundations on which you can build a new life.

However, it is time now to really begin taking the steps on your journey of recovery. The first of these is simply; you need to commit. Commit and admit actually. Or, to be completely correct; admit and commit. You need to admit to yourself that you are suffering from social anxiety. Say it aloud or write it down, it doesn't matter which, but you need to acknowledge it directly.

Actually, it would have, possibly, been more correct to say that you need to admit, accept and then commit, because the next thing you need to do after acknowledging that you have social anxiety is to accept it. We have proven that it is a disorder which can, as the result of a chemical imbalance in the brain or extenuating circumstances like bullying, happen to anyone, and so, it is something that is not your fault. So, you can, and must, forgive yourself for having social anxiety. Yes, seriously.

Again, this might seem embarrassing or cheesy, but you need to say aloud or write down the following; "I forgive myself for suffering from social anxiety. It is not my fault."

It is not something that you asked for or brought on yourself, but instead it is an unwelcome visitor in your life. It is not your fault, and does not have to be part of who you are, so really allow yourself to mean it when you say that you forgive yourself.

In fact, think about your disorder in the way it was described above. "It" was almost personified. "It" was referred to as a multi-faceted, malignant presence that completely dominated the sufferer's life. This is how you should view your social anxiety; as a presence that is almost alive, putting obstacles in your way, and ultimately, something that you will have to overcome if you want to be happy.

This leads to the commitment you need to make. You need to fully embrace this book and follow the steps it outlines, and do so because you know it will help you overcome your social anxiety and regain control of your life. Put this commitment in writing so that you are more likely to stick to it, so write down the following:

I _____ will follow all of the steps in the course, and I will conquer my social anxiety and take control of my life.

Be serious about this oath, hang it up in your room, or put it somewhere you will see it everyday. It is a promise to yourself.

Rejection Therapy

Social anxiety centers around a crippling fear of public settings and the rejection/humiliation that they might entail, so, unsurprisingly one of the fundamental ways to contest this is to confront it head on. Can you feel your heart rate rising already? Are you starting to panic and thinking that this book might be better used as a fan with which to cool yourself? If so, you have probably just realized what the beginning of your recovery calls for.

Don't panic though, you will not be thrown in the figurative deep-end without preparation, you will be using rejection theory yes, but you can start small.

Rejection theory was devised in 2009 by Jason Connelly, and it has five simple, but useful, objectives:

- To increase an awareness of how our lives are controlled and restricted by irrational social fears.
- To take the power away from these fears, and subsequently reap the rewards (yes, these do include better relationships, more self confidence and improved career prospects).
- To stop fearing, and in fact, start learning from, and even enjoying, rejection.
- To stop being so attached to potential outcomes, especially ones that involve things beyond our control, like the free agency of others.
- To allow yourself to fail, and to forgive yourself for failing.

You can think of this form of therapy as a game, and a game with one simple rule: You must be rejected by someone else every single day.

For the purposes of our course, we will be undertaken a 30 day rejection therapy challenge, and, you guessed it, this means that you have to be rejected by somebody different every single day for 30 days. Again, don't stress. You can start small in order to build up your courage and resilience, and in turn you will also be building your confidence and reducing your fear. However, from day one, you need to be rejected face to face, and out of your comfort zone. This means that asking your mother if she wants a cup of coffee when you know she is going to decline does not count!

Here are a few suggestions for rejections as you progress:

In your first few days:

- Try asking retailers if they have sizes/items you think it is unlikely for them to have.
- Ask drivers on public transport if they stop anywhere nearer to your house than where you normally get off.
- Ask a friend to join you on an activity they normally wouldn't enjoy.

As you get braver:

Ask for discounts in a shop before you buy something.

Enticing a girl/guy to ask you for your number.

Ask if you could do some unpaid work experience relating to a profession that you would love to get involved in.

By the final few days:

Start up a conversation with a stranger (perhaps in a book or record store), and ask them to go for coffee with you.

Inquire, face to face, about a job that you would love to have, but that you don't feel you are qualified for.

Ask someone who you feel is out of your league to do something with you. (It doesn't have to be a date, you could invite them to a party your friend is having).

How To Deal With Social Anxiety

The Reasoning

This is not just some risky game designed solely to stretch you boundaries however, there is method to the madness. The science behind the game is quite simple, but it is valid. As has been proven beyond doubt, your mind is like a muscle, and the more you use it, the more you improve it. This extends beyond traditional education and stimulating games like sudoku though, it works with your disposition as well.

In the same way that by hiding in your comfort zone and avoiding social situations you increase the fear and anxiety you feel when forced to interact, by making yourself face rejection consistently, you are building up your bravery. You can think of these exercises in facing fear and rejection exactly like any other workout, except this one is designed to build your courage. And, just as with any other workout, as you progress, you will need heavier weights in order to challenge yourself. This is why it is okay to begin with the easy tasks from the list above, but it is important to move onto more challenging ones in order to continuously push yourself.

Conversely, we can consider how this works with relation to an example that we are all familiar with; Isolation. This can be taken without its negative connotations, and just understood as the time we spend alone. It is something that, in moderation, is enjoyable and important, but this was not always the case. Remember when you were a child, Home Alone movie fantasies aside, if your parents left you in the house by yourself you would have been terrified. And, losing them in a crowded public place was enough to make you break down in tears, but, as we get older, we become more independent. We start to experience having time to ourself, perhaps just playing outside unsupervised, then maybe having a sleep over somewhere and eventually spending an hour or two in the house while everyone else is out. Little by little, your anxiety subsided, and eventually you become comfortable with being the only one home.

The same premise applies to conquering your fear of rejection, eventually things that you considered terrifying won't phase you at all, and, as you become more comfortable, you realize that hearing the word "No" isn't the end of the world. As your confidence improves you will actually start to embrace the word "No", because it makes you stronger every time.

Recovering and Rediscovering

We have begun the initial stage of your recovery through your acceptance and commitment, and have set up the framework for your journey with the 30 day rejection therapy challenge, but it is now time to delve into the main body of work. These are steps to be taken during the 30 day challenge, they compliment it and enhance it, and, will in turn be complimented and enhanced by it.

You can choose your own schedule to follow, but you must have completed all of the steps by the time the 30 days are up if you want to see some real progress. It will be hard and intimidating, you will be pushed far out of your comfort zone and awaken emotions and memories that you have suppressed, but this is all for your own good. Whenever you feel like giving up and letting your social anxiety control you, remember the commitment you made, and remember why you made it.

The Five Pillars of Treatment

There are five main stations on the journey through your treatment:

1) Redirecting Your Thinking
2) Learning to Control Your Breath
3) Facing Your Fears
4) Building Better Relationships
5) Changing Your Lifestyle

They are the pillars of your recovery, and should be moved through in step.

1) Redirecting Your Thinking

Negative thoughts that stem from and, in turn, fueling a distorted world view are one of the fundamental contributors to social anxiety disorder. If you are suffering, you will undoubtedly be familiar with intrusive and destructive thoughts like "*I know I'm going to embarrass myself*", "*My voice, hands, feet or body is going to fail me know*", "*I'm not cool or interesting enough to be here*" etc...

In order to combat the disorder, you need to start challenging these thoughts. This can be done with the help of a therapist, but it can also be done by yourself.

The first step is to recognize irrational, negative thoughts when you have them. For example, when you have a presentation coming and think "*I'm not good enough to do this, I'm going to blow it*". Once you flag these thoughts, think about them and challenge them. In this case, you clearly are good enough to give the presentation or you wouldn't be in the position, and, even if you are nervous when you speak, that doesn't mean that people will see you as incompetent.

Once you have begun to challenge these basic negative thoughts, you can then work on redirecting your thinking. At first this will be challenging, but with practice it will begin to feel natural. People with social anxiety disorder often waste time on the following follies:

Mind Reading: Assuming that you know what others are thinking, and specifically, assuming that they are thinking negative thoughts about you. No disrespect, but they probably have other things on their minds.

Predicting the (Negative) Future: Assuming that things will go horribly wrong before they even happen. This will make you anxious about situations before they begin.

Dramatization: Blowing things out of proportion, i.e thinking that if you wear the wrong thing to school everybody will judge you and your life will be ruined forever. It won't. People won't care, and if they do, they will have forgotten by the next day.

Personalization: Assuming that other people's reactions relate to you in some way. For example, thinking that someone isn't going to a party just because you are attending. Again, no disrespect, but you're probably not that big of a concern to them.

Once you are aware of these thought patterns, you can acknowledge them and put a stop to them. Do not let yourself indulge such fantasies, they are simultaneously narcissistic and inhibiting, and that is not a good combination.

Just being aware of these pitfalls isn't always enough to overcome them ofcourse, so here is some proven advice for getting over the feeling that everyone is watching you:

- Reduce your self focus by giving attention instead to things that are going on around you; look at other people and the surroundings rather than thinking about your own actions and bodily symptoms of anxiety.
- Don't always feel the need to make conversation. Not all silence is awkward, and if you take a minute, someone else will say something.
- Really listen to what is happening around you (either conversation wise or background noise like the radio) instead of focusing on your negative thoughts.

2) Controlling Your Breathing

When you start to feel anxious, your body is overwhelmed by a number of physical symptoms which then make you panic even more. One of the most universal of these is an increase in the speed that you breathe. Breathing too fast throws off the balance of oxygen and carbon dioxide in your body, and this gives rise to other symptoms of anxiety such as dizziness, fast and heavily pounding heart beat, and muscle and facial tension.

Practice the following breathing exercise to lower your breathing speed and stay calm in stressful social situations:

- Sit/stand comfortably with your shoulders relaxed and your back straight.
- Inhale slowly through your nose for four seconds.
- Hold the breath in for two seconds.

- Exhale slowly from your mouth for six seconds, pushing out as much air as possible.
- Continue this steady pattern and focus on it.

3) Facing Your Fears

You will already be doing this on a daily basis with the rejection therapy challenge, but the next step is to overcome your fear of specific social situations. To do this, you need to face the kind of events you would normally avoid head on. Treat them as a challenge to be conquered, and understand that it is your avoidance that perpetuates your social anxiety. Once you embrace these situations, the fear will lose all of its power over you.

Avoidance will also prevent you from reaching your goals and achieving what you are truly capable of. Think about it, you could be an amazing song writer and musician, but unless you show people your ideas, no one will ever appreciate it.

Again, like rejection therapy, this is to be approached in stages. Don't tackle your fears straight away, but work up to them in steps. For example, if you are afraid of meeting new people, go with a friend to a party, or even just spend your lunch break with them in the company of others. When you get comfortable with this, then you can try to talk with the other people in similar situations more directly, and eventually, you will be able to go to places by yourself and have conversations with people you have never met before.

Also, use the skills you have learned in other steps to control your breathing, challenge your negative thoughts and stay calm.

4) Build Better Relationships

Actively engaging in encouraging social environments is another excellent way of conquering social anxiety disorder. By finding inviting and non-intimidating social activities to take part in, you will be able to interact with people without putting yourself under extreme amounts of pressure.

Some examples of these include:

- **Social Skills/Assertive Training Classes:** These are offered in many local schools and colleges as night courses. Not only will they help you to improve your confidence and social skills, they will allow you to mix with people who are struggling in the same way as you, and thus, provide you with an excellent support network.

- **Volunteer Work in Something You Enjoy:** It could be helping out in an animal shelter or putting up posters for a band, what matters is getting out and doing something in an area that interests you while getting to meet like-minded people.

- **Taking Hobby Classes:** If you like to draw, take up an art class. If you like reading, join a book club or even a creative writing class. Again, the goal here is to stimulate and develop your interests in the company of people who are doing the same thing.

5) Change Your Lifestyle

A healthier lifestyle can seriously help your recovery. Your body is fueled by food and maintained by sleep and exercise, so it is little wonder that these elements have a huge impact on how it functions. Make positive changes, and you will soon experience the benefits.

- **Limit Your Caffeine Intake:** Caffeine stimulates your body by sending it in to a state of panic, and unsurprisingly this increases the symptoms of anxiety. Tea, coffee, energy drinks, soda and even some chocolate bars contain high amounts of caffeine and should be avoided as much as possible.

- **Rethink Your Drinking:** In the short term drinking can seem like a way of calming your nerves in social events, but in the long run it can lead to an abundance of mental health issues and increase your levels of anxiety. Even people without social anxiety often report suffering from "The Fear" after a night of heavy drinking!

- **Stop Smoking:** Nicotine is a powerful stimulant, and, despite common misconceptions, after the immediate act or smoking, your anxiety levels will have risen, not lowered.

- **Get Enough Sleep:** Sleeping repairs your brain, and you should get 8 hours a night. If you do not get enough sleep you will be far more vulnerable to anxiety. As the old saying goes "Tiredness makes cowards of us all".

- **Get Some Exercise:** Do not underestimate the importance of regular exercise. Even 30 minutes a day will transform your well being, and a healthy body really does lead to a healthy mind. Also, exercise has the additional benefit of releasing endorphins, these are chemicals in your brain that make you feel happy and relaxed.

Acknowledging and Confronting Your Fears

We have talked about the importance of facing your fears as one of the five pillars of your treatment, and you should be doing this in some way everyday as part of rejection therapy, so you are probably wondering why we are devoting another section to it?

Well, the reason is this: Your disorder is one that centers almost entirely around irrational fear. It may sound harsh and demanding, but the crux of your recovery is based on confronting and overcoming that fear. Any therapist will tell you the same, except they will charge you a lot more!

You need to acknowledge, understand and conquer the things that spark your anxiety. So, without delay, right now, without reading any further, you need to make a list of ten social situations that you are afraid of. Get a pen and paper and start writing. Do not be apprehensive, this is an extremely exciting moment. You are getting ready for a battle, initiating change, and about to regain control of your life.

If you are having trouble focusing at first, take a look at the following suggestions, but make sure to personalize them and add your own.

- Meeting new people
- Being in the center of attention
- Being watched while doing work
- Engaging in small talk
- Public speaking
- Performing on stage
- Being teased or criticized
- Talking with authority figures
- Being asked a question in class
- Going on a date

- Talking on the phone
- Using public bathrooms
- Taking exams
- Eating or drinking in public
- Speaking up in a meeting
- Going to parties or other social events

You should be proud of yourself for taking immediate action and creating your list, it shows determination and dedication, but the work doesn't simply stop there. That's okay though, nothing worth having comes easy.

You now need to to take your list and, at the end of each situation write a score. This score is from a scale of 1-10, regarding how frightening each activity seems to you, with 10 being terrifying and un-achievable, and 1 being something you could do right now without any problems (there shouldn't be any 1's on your score card... yet).

Next, as your confidence improves and you face your fears bit by bit, in the way outlined above, you need to document each stage. For example, if you are terrified of performing on stage or in front of a crowd, but you like to play music, start by playing to a friend. Casually play something and ask what they think. Before doing so, write down how scared the thought made you feel, and then after you have done it, write down another score correlating to how scary it seems to you now. The second score will be much lower. Continue this as you face your fear in steps, for example, you might next play in front of your family, then you can try to play with a band... and eventually you will be able to get up on stage and play.

Keep these lists, they are the markers of your recovery. Constantly push your boundaries, and as you see how the before score is much higher than the after score, you will not only realize that irrational fear is at the root of your problem, you will defeat it. And, finally, when you have faced your fears, rewrite a new overall score beside the initial one. It will be much lower, because you will be much more confident.

Taking Action

Call to Action

Okay, so you have bought this book and are following the steps, good for you. However, if you are not 100% dedicated you are wasting your time. You cannot be just interested in self improvement, you need to be fully committed. And yes, there is a difference. Interest reads this book but makes excuses and procrastinates, commitment follows its steps through with a clear focus, and constantly pushes boundaries and acquires new skills.

This book provides you with the raw materials to turn your life around, but it cannot make the changes for you. The knowledge and advice offered to you here is powerful and transforming, but just reading it won't help. You need to apply it fully, and follow it no matter how anxious you feel. Unless, of course, you want to regress and to continue living in fear.

Do you want to continue living a life governed by fear?

Do you want to wake up one day, old and unfulfilled, having watched your years slip by without having mastered your own destiny and achieved what you are capable of? With nothing to show for your time here on earth and your potential left as a "What if" or "If only..."?

Or

Do you want to take control and experience the full, rich life that you deserve?

Of course you do, who wouldn't want to make that change, but the question is; how badly do you want it?

Do you want to take control and master your own life more than you want to avoid being embarrassed? More than you want to hide away at home playing videos games or watching TV?

More than you want to keep from putting yourself out there and risk failing?

More than you want to get drunk and experience some short term solution?

Think about it, seriously, these are your options. You can stay safe in your comfort zone, or you can make real changes that will help you direct the course of your life to somewhere that you want it to go.

Yes, it is scary, and you will feel anxious and panic in the moment, but remember, if you only look after your short term self, your long term self will suffer.

If you ever feel like giving up, take the advice offered by Harvey Firestein: "Never be bullied into silence. Never allow yourself to be less then you can be. Accept no one's definition of your life, instead, define yourself".

Setting Your Goals

What
The only way you are going to get to where you want to be in your life is by knowing exactly where it is that you want to go.

Obviously this does not have to be a literal journey or progression, but it does have to relate to what you want to achieve. Whether you want to be in a big office in a new job, or just in a position to walk into a shop without feeling anxious, you need to define exactly what it is that you want to accomplish in order to have a clear goal to work towards.

Think about everything that you want to achieve as part of your recovery, and everything that you want to do once you have regained control of your life.

These goals can be simple like the second example above. You may want to:

- Answer a question in class
- Suggest an idea at work
- Go to a party
- Talk to someone you are attracted to
- Go to a movie with a group of friends
- Order a takeaway over the phone
- Make contact with a long lost friend

Or, they can be more long term like the first example. These could include:

- Having the courage to move away next year for work or college
- Putting yourself forward for a promotion
- Starting a blog, and promoting it to people you know
- Taking control of a creative project
- Being able to make a move on your long term crush
- Taking time off to go and travel

You should set both short term and long term goals, and treat your small term successes as triumphant steps toward your long term plan.

How

It is no use just setting a goal without a plan of action. You need a strategy, a game plan, a way of making your dream a reality. Think about what you want to achieve, and then think about how you are going to approach it.

There is no sure way to do this, as every goal is different, but there are some universal things that you can do to realize your aspirations.

Preparation is the key. Ever heard the saying *"Fail to prepare, prepare to fail"*? Well, it rings true in every aspect of life. From simple goals to long term dreams, putting the time and effort into getting ready is what will help you to capitalize on opportunities. This could be something as fundamental as making a new friend, if you want to talk to someone but are nervous about having a conversation, plan what you are going to say ahead of time. And, in the long term, all of your smaller successes will have helped you to prepare and build your confidence so that you can embrace the changes for bigger chances when they come.

Accept that setbacks will happen, but do not give up. It is unlikely that all your endeavors will be successful the very first time you try them, but you must not give up. Giving up is the only real way of failing. If you want to be a member of a military army, but on your first tryout you fail the fitness test, you need to go back to the drawing board (and the dressing room), and work on getting yourself in shape for the next tryout. If you do this, but then fail the interview on your next attempt, you then need to go back and work on your interview skills. Persistence is the key to success.

Ultimately, you have to think rationally and realistically about how to achieve your goals. If your life ambition is to be a movie director, consider the ways in which you can make this happen, and make them into a plan. First you may want to get some equipment and experience. Then, while you are working on projects you can focus on developing your communication skills as well as you creative ones. Don't be afraid to look for advice from writings on the subject or directly from people involved in the industry. When you have built up enough knowledge, you can start being more ambitious, and try to get involved in some bigger projects. From here, try to get noticed. Submit your work to competitions and professional studios, eventually you will get where you want to be.

Of course, this is just an example, but whether you want to be the manager of a big company, a writer or a race car driver, the same step by step method applies. After all, no matter how big the meal, the only way to eat is one mouthful at a time.

When

Your approach needs to be disciplined. This is how you will remain driven and motivated. It is of no use having a goal and a plan of action without a time frame. You need to set yourself deadlines. When setting out to achieve your goals, decide when you want each step of the plan to be completed by.

For example, if you are terrified of public speaking but want to take part in a debate, pick a time that you aim to be able to do this by. Let's say 6 months, that gives you ample time to prepare. But, start small. Maybe say that by the end of the second week of this time frame you want to ask a question in class, and, by the following week, you want to answer one. Then maybe a month down the line from that you will have taken part in a few group discussions. Over the next month, do some group presentations, and then move on to doing solo ones. You have been given the techniques to keep calm while doing so as the pillars of your treatment, and once you get some experience applying these, you will build the confidence necessary not just to take part in a debate, but to master it.

Staying Focused

Phenomenal people like Croix Sather, who holds a world record for running across America, are where they are today because they possess a do or die attitude. This means that when they decide to do something, they commit to that goal no matter what. They are willing to do whatever it takes to succeed, and know that sometimes it will be uncomfortable, sometimes it will be hard and sometimes it will be scary. But, because they want it bad enough, they will keep going despite all the difficulties. And, because of that, they will get there in the end.

This is the kind of attitude that you must develop if you want to change your life. There can be no half measures. You need to be focused and driven. Of course, that is easier said than done initially, so here are some tips to get you off on the right foot:

- Forgive yourself if you make mistakes. Nobody is perfect, you won't always stick to your plan. When this happens, don't waste time feeling bad, pick yourself up and do not make the same mistake next time.

- Focus on your motivation when you feel like giving up. There will be times when you want to quit and revert to the old ways, but remember what you want to achieve, and why you want to achieve it.

- Make things easy on yourself by following the steps you have set out. Don't try too much at once.

- Find enjoyment in what you are doing. If you are trying to be more social, do it in contexts that you enjoy. For example, if you don't like sports, don't force yourself to go and mix at a sporting event, do it somewhere you feel comfortable instead. This could be a game shop, art class or cooking workshop.

Take Responsibility

You need to make yourself accountable. This will work as strong motivation, and encourage you to try again if you fail at first.

There are a number of ways you can do this:

Setting up a Goal System:

You have already listed your top ten fears and should be working towards conquering them. Once you have begun to do this you can start moving directly toward your goals. We have talked above about the importance of clearly defined goals with plans of actions and time frames, but it is now time to chart them.

Think about everything that you want to achieve. You should never stop wanting to improve, so this is an ongoing task, but for now, come up with 5 short term and 5 long term goals. These can be similar to the ones offered as examples above, or completely different, what matters is that they are things you want to do. Well, they are now on your to do list, and making to do lists of things that you want to accomplish are one of the universal secrets of highly successful people.

You should divide your notebook into two sections, one for long term goals and one for short term goals. For your short term goals, give yourself a time period of around two weeks. By this time you should have accomplished everything you have set out to, and will be able to add 5 more things. Like your rejection therapy, these should increase in ambition every time, but unlike the rejection therapy challenge, you should keep it up for much longer than 30 days. Your long term goals, obviously, will take a lot longer to move through, they can be things six months or so ahead, or life long ambitions. Either, or anywhere between is fine, but make sure that you write a time frame beside each goal. Add to this list liberally, as you progress, you will be pleasantly surprised at how many you cross off.

For each goal, also write your plan of action. An example of two complete goal system entries could look like this:

Short Term Goals:
- Answer question in class;
  - Read over class material so I will know the answers.
  - Decide on the class, use breathing techniques before answering and challenge negative thoughts/avoid feeling overly self conscious by focusing on what is going on in the class after.

Long Term Goals:
- Be the center of attention at a party in 6 months time (without needing alcohol);
  - First, get over my fear of going to parties.
  - Next, get more comfortable talking to people.
  - Finally, prepare a funny story or joke to tell at party in front of a group of people.

Tell Family and Friends:
While this can be extremely hard to do at first, once you confide in your family and friends you will be surprised at how supportive they are. When they learn that you are trying to improve yourself, they will be understanding and helpful. Don't be embarrassed when telling people your goals, you are doing an extremely positive thing. In ten years down the line, it won't matter that you

needed a little help now, it will only matter that you took control of your life and got to a place that you wanted to be.

The real benefit of this however, is the extra motivation that if offers. Once people know about what you are trying to achieve they will not only encourage you, they will push you. You will regularly be asked to provide proof of your progress. For example, if you are trying to get better at going to public places, your family might insist you join them for an outing, this is a good thing! Furthermore your supporters will not let you quit. There is no shame in failing on an attempt, but there is shame in giving up. If this happens, use the judgement and scorn of others to fuel your determination.

Find People on Similar Journeys:

Just like people going to the gym benefit from having workout partners to keep them focused, your recovery will benefit from having someone to share it with. Find people who want to achieve similar things than you do, and work with them.

Having them to guide you and offer you support will help you through the hard times, and returning the favor by helping them will also be extremely rewarding. You could team up with a friend or family member who also exhibits symptoms of social anxiety, meet someone at the social skills or related classes offered in community centers or even just visit an online support group, there are plenty of them.

Conclusion

Well, there you have it. You have read through this entire book of tried and tested advice to help you to conquer your social anxiety. Congratulations. But, of course, this is only the beginning. You now have the information, but it is up to you to act upon it. You can do it though, you have everything you need.

Let's recap everything you have learned.

First, it was necessary for you to define social anxiety disorder, to consider its symptoms and to see if you were really suffering from it. Then, it was important to reach a more in-depth understanding of the disorder, and to know that you are not the only one who feels the way you do, and, that you feel the way you do because of your mental condition, not because there is something fundamentally wrong with you.

It is possible to overcome social anxiety, and once you realized that, it was time to begin your recovery. This can be now broken down into five simple steps:

1. **Admit, Accept, Commit:** Before anything could happen you needed to admit that you had social anxiety. Forgive yourself for it, and commit to doing whatever it takes to regain command of your life.

2. **30 Day Rejection Therapy Challenge:** Although your journey will extend far beyond this period of time, this is extremely important first step. You learned to face your fear of rejection, and that doing so wasn't as terrible as you thought.

3. **5 Pillars of Treatment:** These are the basic tools that will help you to overcome social anxiety. When applied to rejection therapy and the other challenges, it will make things much easier and more achievable.

4. **Setting Goals:** Creating your system of clearly defined goals, with strategies and deadlines for each is no easy task, but it is extremely worthwhile. Having your aspirations in writing will keep you focused, motivated, driven and organized. This is your to do list, enjoy ticking things off of it.

5. **Taking Action/Taking Responsibility:** *"Everybody dreams, some people just wake up and work hard to make those dreams become reality"*. You need to take action. This guide will only work if you put it into practice. Make yourself accountable, answer to your to do list, your family/friends and your support network.

With that, you are not only ready to take action and take responsibility, you are ready to take control. Control of your social anxiety, control of the direction of your life and control of your own destiny.

To leave you with the simple but powerful words of George Elliot:

"It is never too late to be who you might have been".

The Story of Jia Jiang

Yes, you have finished reading the book's program, but as an added bonus, here is the entertaining and inspiring story of Jia Jiang; a man who overcame his fears and transformed his life as result, and owes it all to rejection therapy.

Many years ago, Jia Jiang travelled far from his native land, and moved to the United States of America, with the lofty dream of being the next Bill Gates. However, despite his potential and some promising early success in the corporate world, his first attempt at pursuing his dreams of entrepreneurial extravagance ended in rejection. Jia was devastated. His once unflinching self belief and swaggering confidence were shaken, and he descended into an anxious state of self doubt and depression. And, as I'm sure you will believe, there are not many socially anxious entrepreneurs.

Unable to bring himself to undertake any other projects, he had all but given up on his dream, when the revelation hit him. He realized that what was holding him back was not a lack of talent or shortage of ideas, it was actually his fear of rejection itself. That is what made him so nervous the first time around, and that is what was preventing him from getting anything else off the ground. Once he was aware of this, he could clearly see that it was his fear of rejection that was the biggest obstacle in the way of his success, and why fear being rejected if you aren't even going to put your self out there! He knew that he needed to find a way of coping with the word "No" otherwise it would ruin his dreams. This gave birth to his 100 Day Rejection Challenge, which follows the exact same principle as Rejection Therapy; the best way to conquer a fear of rejection is to face it head on, and so, he set out to be told "No" by a stranger once a day, for 100 hundred days!

His ideas were very amusing, and are potentially useful for anyone still taking the 30 Day Challenge. They include asking a stranger for a loan of $100, bringing his tire in to get dry cleaned and asking a car salesman to give him a lesson on how to deliver a pitch. During this time, he actually learned how to get people to agree to ridiculous requests just by asking in a certain way (seriously, he has gotten to make announcements over the speaker on an airplane and received Krispy Kreme donuts in the shape of Olympic rings. More importantly however, he developed the skills necessary to cope with being rejected and managed to build his confidence so that now his plans cannot be derailed by single setbacks.

Having written a successful book about his experiences and been invited to speak on many high profile platforms (including Ted Talks and web Summits), Jia is now living his dream. And, as he says himself, if it can happen to him, it can happen to you.

Table of Contents

Made in the USA
Las Vegas, NV
12 December 2021

37242995R00033